I0061604

MILLINERY FOR MISSES AND CHILDREN

Copyright © 2013 Read Books Ltd.
This book is copyright and may not be
reproduced or copied in any way without
the express permission of the publisher in writing

British Library Cataloguing-in-Publication Data
A catalogue record for this book is available from the
British Library

Millinery

Whereas 'hatmaking' is the manufacture of hats and headwear, 'millinery' also encompasses the *designing* and manufacture of hats. A milliner's store, predictably, is a shop which sells those goods. Historically, milliners, typically female shopkeepers, produced or imported an inventory of garments for men, women, and children, including hats, shirts, cloaks, shifts, caps, neckerchiefs, and undergarments, and sold these garments in their millinery shop. More recently, the term has evolved to refer specifically to someone who designs and makes hats, usually primarily for a female clientele. The origin of the term is likely the Middle English *milener*, an inhabitant of Milan or one who deals in items from this Italian city, known for its fashion and clothing.

Many styles of headgear have been popular through history and worn for different functions and events. They can be part of uniforms or worn to indicate social status. Styles include the top hat, hats worn as part of military uniforms, cowboy hat, and cocktail hat. Perhaps the most recent popular incarnation is the fascinator; a style which uses feathers, stylish materials, beads, pearls and crystals - ranging from extravagant to petite for brides, weddings, christenings, ladies' day at the horse races and many other glamorous occasions.

Notable Milliners include the German born Anna Ben-Yusuf (1845-1909), who wrote *The Art of Millinery* (1909), one of the first reference books on millinery technique. It was formatted as a series of lessons, each dealing with a particular aspect of constructing a hat, treating the fabric or creating different types of trimming. Ben-Yusuf also set up her own school of millinery, based in Boston and New York. On a more practical note, it also advised on correct storage, renovating fabrics, and the business side of millinery, and included a glossary of terms. Subsequently, milliners such as Lilly Daché have achieved notable success. This French designer made hats for many Hollywood films and movie stars, including Marlene Dietrich, Caroline Lombard and Loretta Young. Her major contributions to millinery were draped turbans, brimmed hats molded to the head, half hats, visored caps for war workers, coloured snoods, and romantic massed-flower shapes.

Today, designers such as Philip Treacy and Stephen Jones are at the forefront of the millinery profession. Jones especially is considered one of the world's most radical and important milliners, also one of the most prolific, having created hats for the catwalk shows of many leading couturiers and fashion designers, such as John Galliano at Dior and Vivienne Westwood. His work is known for its inventiveness and the high level of technical expertise with which he realises his ideas.

MILLINERY FOR MISSES AND CHILDREN

ESSENTIALS OF APPROPRIATE JUVENILE MILLINERY

1. In accordance with the trend of time, hats for growing girls and tiny tots are receiving just as much attention as those for grown-ups. Whole establishments are now given over to the making of misses' hats, and clever designers are devoting all their time and inventive powers to this particular branch of millinery. The result is that enough charming and varied designs are produced to suit every youthful type without resorting to eccentricities, which very often make the young girl look ridiculous.

To create appropriate juvenile fashions, the designer must possess a wide understanding of children from the toddling age to budding misses in their teens and must be able to appreciate the feelings, habits, and desires of girlhood. In addition, the successful designer must possess the ability to impart the spirit of youth to the resulting creations by the turn of a brim, the tilt of a quill, or the perk of a bow.

In spite of the production of styles that are distinctly for children, so broad is its scope that the line of demarcation in millinery between that worn by the juvenile and that worn by big sister and mother, has never been less defined than at present. Therefore, the same general principles governing the designing and developing of hats for adults are applicable in the construction of hats for juveniles.

2. Range of Juvenile Millinery.—Millinery for children begins with the tiny tots who have just outgrown their soft bonnets and whose little curls are peeping underneath the brim of their first real hat. For this age, a soft hat without any wires or stiff frames that are likely to hurt the child's head, is developed to look just a wee bit like those of her older sisters whose ages run from four to

COPYRIGHTED BY INTERNATIONAL EDUCATIONAL PUBLISHING COMPANY. ALL RIGHTS RESERVED eight years. These sisters, also, require an equal amount of attention in the selection of hats with the head-size a little larger, the brim a trifle different, and the style in general somewhat older than that worn by the more youthful members of the family.

Then come the misses who are in their early teens and who need a hat or two for school and one for "Sunday best." As these young misses advance to their teen age and begin to take an active part in the various athletic sports of their preference, they require smart sports hats, with matching scarfs or sweaters, for such occasions.

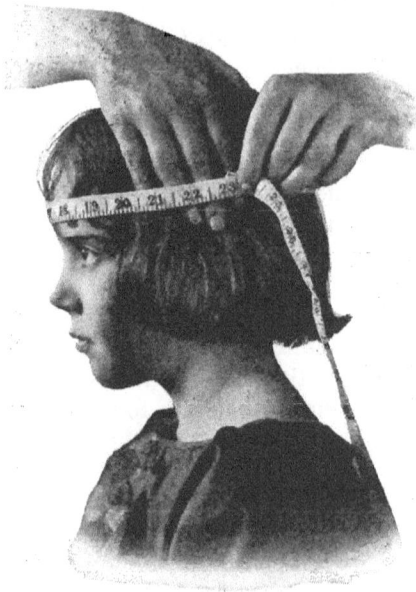

So, the range in millinery for children and misses is wider than would at first thought be supposed. But whether the hat is for the very youngest tot in the family or for big sister of grade-school age, it should be characterized by the three requisites of children's millinery,—comfort, simplicity, and becoming-ness,—and its brim, crown, fabric, color, and trimming should be appropriate for the type of child and the use to be made of the hat.

FIG. 1

3. Comfort in Children's Hats.—Comfort is essential in every branch of millinery, but it is particularly important in hats for young folks. Nothing is more annoying and consequently disturbing to a child's disposition than a hat that is too tight or one that does not fit the head properly. To produce a hat that will give the greatest degree of comfort, the head-size must be just right.

In fact, the head-size, the beginning of all hats, is one of the most important factors in millinery for children and deserves considerable attention. Even the blocked hats of straw and felt show a pronounced tendency toward softness at the head-size.

In hats for the tiny tots, the head-sizes are governed by their years, but, in those for juveniles over four years old, the head-size measure must be known. To obtain the correct measurement of the head-size of a miss, use the same method as for a grown-up; that is, run the tape line around the head just above the eyebrows, over the top of the ears, and around the back of the head, as shown in Fig. 1, holding it sufficiently loose to permit the insertion of the fingers between the tape and the head. Then, measure from ear to ear, as shown in Fig. 2, in order to determine the cor-

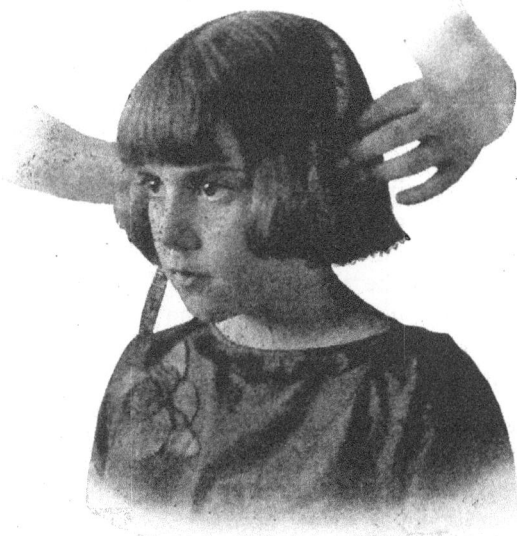

FIG. 2

rect measurement of the depth of the crown and prevent the buying of a hat too small or one that comes too far down on the head.

4.   Simplicity of Style.—Good taste is just as dominant a factor in juvenile millinery as in that for grown-ups. So the mother should endeavor to cultivate a desire for simplicity in the girl at an early age. Too often young folks are influenced by types of hats worn by their favorite movie star, but these designs, which are usually extreme and theatrical in order to attract public fancy, are in no way a safe guide for the growing girl.

On the other hand, the line of the hat and the kind of material and trimming used should possess an air of youthful simplicity.

Very often the same hat may be suitable for old and young, but to be worn by a girl in her teens or younger it must have just the right lines and carry its trimming so as to accentuate these lines.

Producing simplicity in hats is usually a question of the proper balancing of the parts and the trimming so as to prevent an overloaded appearance. For instance, if a tam is drawn down on the right side in the usual manner, some sort of cocarde, ribbon bow, or ornament should be applied on the left as a balance. The art of knowing how to balance a hat is not acquired all at once, but comes with constant practice and study.

5. Becomingness.—In the development of children's hats, becomingness is sometimes overshadowed by the desire on the part of the mother to purchase or make a hat that will be entirely practical and serviceable. The time has passed when the conventional, but ever-becoming, poke was considered the only proper hat for every little girl. Now, there is a different type of hat for every junior feminine head, and all must be fitted and adjusted until they are just right in size and line. Then, the material and the trimming should be chosen of a kind and a color that will further enhance the good qualities of the wearer and subdue the poor ones. The completed model cannot help but produce an effect that will be pleasing and thoroughly desirable.

6. Variety in Shape.—Just as in big sister's hats, unlimited variety prevails in the type of shapes. Instead of being restricted to one or two particular types, each new season the juvenile may choose from exact duplicates of the shapes used for grown-up sister. These include the Breton, cloche, chin-chin, soft pull-on, rolled-front toque, large, even-brim shape, and both the broad-of-side and the long, scoop-front poke brim. These characterized by a simplicity that should always be evident in children's hats will produce models of unusual charm.

The crown, too, favors variation, and when Fashion decrees the soft, the semi-soft, or the severely plain type in the adult's hat, the hat of the little miss, also, shows a note of softness in the four-, five-, or six-piece section, unsupported except for a narrow head-size band.

For school and general wear, the tam in two pieces or the many-section biretta, entirely unsupported, cannot be excelled. These tams are worn throughout the year, made in material matching the child's coat in fall and winter, and developed in silk or all-over straw fabric for spring and summer wear.

Next in popularity is the blocked hat of milan, hemp, leghorn, and natural straw for spring and summer, and in felt, beaver, and velours for fall and winter. These blocked hats can be used for school by being trimmed with ribbon bands and scarfs, or for the more dressy occasions by being trimmed with flowers, fruits, and other novelty trimmings.

7. Width of Brim.—In selecting hats for children from five to fourteen years old, the width of the brim is a very essential consideration, because too wide a brim on a short child gives her a submerged appearance to her grown-up sister who, of necessity, looks down on a big hat overshadowing a little girl; while too narrow a brim on a large child gives her an undesirable overgrown appearance. Consequently, it is not the age of a child, but rather her height that determines the size of brim.

8. Proper-Fitting Crown.—The next important factor to be considered in developing hats for growing girls is the crown, as this must make allowances for the way a child's hair is arranged. If a child wears a perky bow on the top of her head, a crown with ample room must be provided. Yet, it sometimes seems as if the manufacturers of blocked hats do not take into consideration the necessity of a proper-fitting crown, and children's hats are turned out with no apparent allowance made for such details as hair ribbons.

9. Fabrics and Colors.—The young girl enjoys the privilege of using all the different fabrics, such as straw cloth, crêpe, taffeta, satin, faille, duvetyn, plush, and brocades, which are displayed for grown-ups, as well as copying the detailed trimming arrangements and colors employed.

Instead of depending on the staple dark blues, browns, reds, tans, light blue, pink, and white of former years, the growing miss may now select brilliant Chinese red, hyacinth blue, mimosa yellow, or cyclamen pink. Even lavender, orchid, and violet tones are now considered appropriate for young girls, especially if they complete a color scheme or are becoming.

10. Suitable Trimmings.—Hats for misses and children should never be overtrimmed, it being better to use too little trimming than too much. A simple, artistic arrangement is much more desirable than an elaborate one, because an overloaded trim is likely to appear top-heavy and unbalanced.

For school or every-day wear, stiffly tailored or pump bows, with or without long-end streamers, are choice. For dress-up models, a rosette bow, a bunch of cherries, a half-wreath of pretty, mixed flowers or fine fruits, an all-around wreath of field flowers, or two or three bunches of flowers applied at irregular intervals, make sufficient trimming at any time.

Probably the simplest form of trimming and one of the most suitable for children's millinery is hand-work. Even the plainest embroidered design or a tiny motif appliquéd on the brim or crown will make a smart poke or a pull-on cuff shape a work of art. Handmade blossoms and flat-embroidered yarn flowers seem to have become "permanently fixed" as a garniture for misses and children's hats. One of the advantages of hand-work is the many unique color effects that are made possible by this sort of trimming.

VARIETIES OF JUVENILE HATS

POKE BONNET

11. Nature of Poke.—A shape that stands out prominently from season to season, and one that is equally becoming to the very youthful, to the growing girl, and to the adult, is the poke shape. This is familiarly called the *poke bonnet*, because of its close-fitting, bonnet-like back, its wide, scooping front, and its sides shaped down over the ears. Formerly, long streamers of ribbon were attached to the sides and, when not allowed to hang over the shoulders, were tied in a bow under the chin.

In recent years, this particular shape has undergone numerous modifications, each new season bringing changes in its contour. For the average growing girl, however, these changes need not have much weight, for if a poke of a certain line is more becoming to her than the particular one that the season's fashion is stressing, she should wear the type that is most becoming. Often, merely a rearrangement of the trimming might give the added touch and produce the new effect that a last season's hat requires.

The frame shown in Fig. 3 is a practical type of poke that is not extreme in outline. It is medium in size and can, with slight alteration, be worn successfully by several different types of girls. One way in which this frame may be developed is shown in Fig. 4. Here it has rather severe lines; that is, the frame is defined or the material applied in a plain, smooth manner, the wide silk scarf being the only softening effect. This type of hat is exceptionally

Fig. 3

appropriate as a sports or a general-utility hat and is especially becoming to a miss whose hair is fluffy or curly.

12. Dimensions.—The dimensions of the brim of this frame are: Head-size, 22 inches; back, 1 inch; front, 3 inches; direct sides, $2\frac{1}{2}$ inches; front diagonal, $2\frac{3}{4}$ inches; back diagonal, 2 inches; edge, 34 inches. The oval crown measures $14\frac{1}{2}$ inches from back to front, and $13\frac{1}{4}$ inches from side to side.

13. Material Requirements.—A 10-yard piece of visca braid about 1 inch wide and $\frac{1}{2}$ yard of 36-inch-wide taffeta silk are the materials used in constructing this model. For the rings, $\frac{1}{8}$ yard of buckram will be needed.

Fig. 4

14. Covering the Brim.—To cover the brim, first bind with the braid. Then, for the top facing, sew the braid spirally from the edge to the head-size. Sew each row of braid firmly to the edge of the preceding one, so that the edges do not overlap but merely come together with no intervening spaces.

Next, apply the under facing of taffeta. Lay the piece of taffeta over the under brim with a corner in the direct front, and pin it on the edge and at the head-size. Next, shape and smooth it around to the center back, working all the fulness to this point. Cut away the surplus material around the edge, at the back, and around the head-size opening, allowing ½ inch for a seam at the back and ¾ inch for slashing around the head-size. Stitch it around the head-size and then slash it, and slip-stitch the seam at the back. Then turn the outer edge of the silk over a wire, and make a cord, or French, finish, as described in Art. **67,** *Elements of Millinery.*

15. Covering the Crown.—To cover the crown, begin to sew the braid spirally at the base in the center back, defining the oval shape and finishing at the center top. Then you are ready to make the rings and drape the taffeta around the crown.

16. Making the Rings.—For these rings, first make a pattern by cutting a piece of paper 4 inches wide and 4½ inches long. Fold it through the middle and round off the corners into a true oval shape; then out of the center cut an oval 2½ inches by 3 inches in diameter. Using this pattern as a guide, cut three circles from the buckram; then wire each edge, as shown at *a*, Fig. 5.

FIG. 5

To cover the buckram foundations, begin on the inner side by attaching one end of the braid and then wind it around the buckram as shown at *b* until the entire piece is covered. Fasten the end neatly by slipping it under one of the rows of braid and tacking it.

17. Applying the Drape.—For the drape, cut a 12-inch-wide bias strip of taffeta, put a rolled hem on each edge, and run the strip through the braid rings. Draw the taffeta around the side crown and adjust the rings an equal distance apart, placing one in the direct front and one on each side, as shown. For a finish, cross the two ends of the drape at the back and tuck them under the taffeta at the sides, making a neat finish and a simple trim suitable for a smart, tailored hat for early spring.

VARIATIONS OF POKE SHAPE

SUMMER MODEL

18. Nature of Hat.—For a dressy, airy, midsummer hat, one that adds the necessary touch to the dainty, summer frock, nothing could be more suitable than the model shown in Fig. 6. Although it is developed on the same foundation frame as the preceding poke, the general contour is changed entirely by the manner in which the fabric is applied.

Overlapping petals fall gracefully over the brim and a balloon crown in crushed effect continues the soft, airy note expressed throughout this summery model. A plaque of fine, dainty flowers trims the front.

Organdie, taffeta, crêpe, or chiffon may be used in developing this model, and the under facing may be of braid or of the same fabric as is used on top. In this particular case, organdie is used for the entire hat.

19. Material Requirements.—A commendable feature about this model is that it can easily be made of small pieces of material that are left over from a frock. The quantity of material used in the hat illustrated is 1 yard of 40-inch organdie. If, however, the hat were to have an additional braid facing, 4 yards of flat braid would be needed besides the yard of organdie.

FIG. 6

20. Covering the Foundation Brim.—To cover the brim, cut a bias strip of the organdie long enough to reach around the edge of the brim and wide enough to reach from the head-size on top over the edge to the head-size underneath, allowing an extra 3 inches for the width that is lost in the bias during the stretching. Stretch this strip firmly around the edge wire to obtain the correct size, cut off the bias corners, and then make a straight, machine-stitched seam in the direct back. Slip the material over the edge wire again and stretch it firmly into the head-size on the top and the under brim. Now hold it over a steaming kettle to remove any extra fulness around the head-size.

If a braid facing is desired, bind the edge with a flat hemp or visca braid and sew this spirally into the head-size after the organdie facing has been applied.

21. Making the Petals.—The next step is to cut the petals. To develop a pattern for the petals, fold through the center lengthwise a piece of tissue paper $4\frac{1}{2}$ inches by 5 inches, making an oblong piece $2\frac{1}{4}$ inches by 5 inches, as shown at view (a), Fig. 7.

About $1\frac{1}{2}$ inches from the top on the open edges, as at a, draw a curved line with the aid of some curved object to about $\frac{3}{4}$ inch from the folded edge, as at b.   Next, beginning on the bottom, $\frac{1}{2}$ inch from the open edge, as at c, taper it off to nothing along the side, as at d, $2\frac{1}{2}$ inches from the bottom edge.   Cut along these lines,

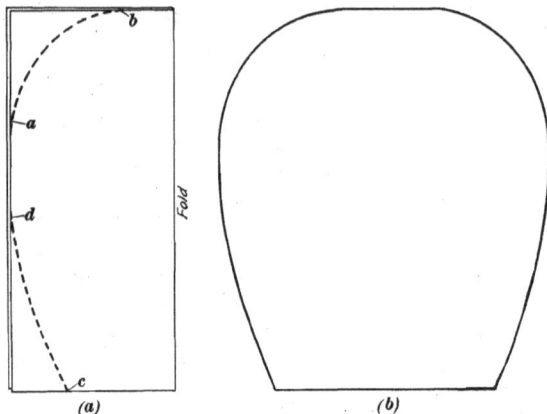

Fig. 7

open out the paper, and the petal will appear as in view (b), Fig. 7. It may be possible that you can gauge the shaping of this pattern with the eye and eliminate the drawing of the lines, but you must be very exact so that the curved portion has an even line.

With this pattern, cut eleven such petals and have them hemstitched about $\frac{1}{2}$ inch from the edge; then, to produce a picot edge, cut through the hemstitching, as shown in Fig. 8, all around the edge of each petal.

22. Applying the Petals.—In applying the petals to the brim, it will be necessary to make two or three $\frac{1}{2}$-inch slashes, as illustrated at a, Fig. 8, in order to make them conform to the shape of the head-size.

Pin the center-front petal in place by pinning it to the center front of the head-size band. Then slip the next petal under the first, as shown in the completed model, and continue graduating them around to the center back, following the outline of the frame. On the opposite side of the brim, apply the petals in the same manner, covering the entire brim and allowing them to extend in a scalloped effect beyond the edge. Trim off any surplus material that may be left over after fitting the petals around the head-size.

23. Covering the Crown.—For the crown illustrated, a two-piece balloon crown is crushed down over the regulation oval foundation. To make this balloon covering, use a circular piece, 7 inches

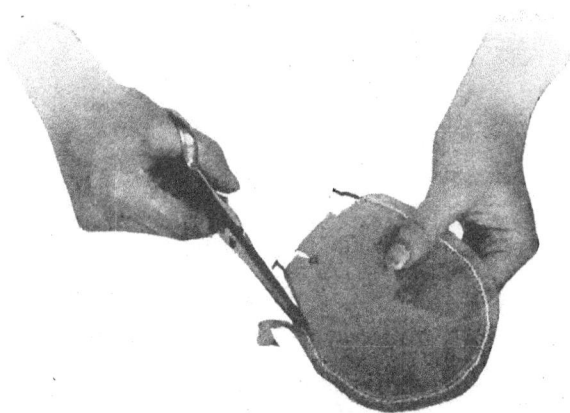

FIG. 8

in diameter, for the tip and machine-stitch to this tip a bias strip, 7 inches wide and 22 inches long, which has previously been joined in a ring.

If a transparent hat is desired, the foundation crown may be omitted and a *cap crown* made by shirring a circle of the organdie 13 inches in diameter around the edge and attaching it to the head-size of the brim. This little cap crown will serve as a foundation for the balloon, which is drawn over it and slip-stitched to the top brim.

To finish the crown, drape the side crown in several folds and tie-stitch it at intervals to the foundation crown or cap.

24. Trimming.—As a trim, appliqué a plaque of fine flowers across the front at the base of the crown. There are, however, numerous other trimming arrangements which may be substituted according to the tastes of the wearer, one of which might be a bow of organdie in the same or in a contrasting color, hemstitched on the edges and sides, and attached at a becoming angle.

WINTER MODEL

25.   Nature of Hat.—In Fig. 9, the preceding model is reproduced in a winter fabric. One yard of duvetyn, broadcloth, velvet, or any material used for the little girl's coat, together with small pieces of lining in the same or a contrasting color, can, with a little hand-work, be transformed into this attractive hat.

26.   Making the Brim.—To make the brim, first cover the under brim of the frame plain with a suitable material, perhaps scraps of

FIG. 9

crêpe de Chine, Canton crêpe or light-weight taffeta left over from lining the coat. Draw the outer edge of the material over the edge of the frame and in about 1 inch on the top. Make the petals of duvetyn or the material selected and face them with whatever forms the under brim. Slip-stitch the edges together and outline them with stitching done in wool. Then, apply them to the brim in graduating sizes, as shown, a full-sized one in front, the rest overlapping and diminishing in size toward the back so as to follow the outline of the poke shape. Allow them to extend in a soft, scalloped effect beyond the edge, as do the organdie petals in the summer model.

27.   Making the Crown.—For the crown, join in a ring a bias strip 9 inches wide on the selvage edge and long enough to fit snugly around the head-size. Run three rows of shirring, 1 inch apart, along one lengthwise edge for the top. Draw these shirr strings up to conform to the shape of the crown and finish at the center top with a covered button mold. Pull this over the foundation crown and slip-stitch around the head-size.

28.   Trimming.—The trimming consists of a hand-made flower spray appliquéd on the side crown at the right-side front. Make the petals of this flower and the leaves of the crêpe or taffeta and outline them with a buttonhole-stitch. Draw a band of narrow ribbon around the base of the crown and tie in a simple two-loop-and-two-end bow at the back.

This completes a hat of matchless charm, particularly appropriate for a demure young miss with rather straight, bobbed hair. The soft edge is more becoming to this type than to the one whose hair is fluffy.

BROAD-OF-SIDES MUSHROOM

ONE-PIECE BLOCKED MODEL

29. Another style of frame that possesses many possibilities is the slightly mushroom droop, wider at the sides than in front and back. The one shown in Fig. 10 is a one-piece blocked shape

FIG. 10

of French felt, which is especially smart for sports or general street wear and decidedly becoming to petite faces. Its trimming continues the youthful simplicity, it being a band of grosgrain ribbon that is finished at the right-side front with a soft, pump bow and a folded cross-knot.

FIG. 11

SECTIONAL WINTER MODEL

30. On the same style of foundation frame, the hat shown in Fig. 11 is developed in a combination of fabrics. Duvetyn is used for the plain-fitted brim and gros de Londres makes the six-piece sectional crown.

31. Foundation Frame.—As a foundation for this model, a frame of the following dimensions is used: Head-size, 23 inches; back, $2\frac{5}{8}$ inches; front, $2\frac{1}{4}$ inches; direct sides, 4 inches; front diagonal, $3\frac{3}{4}$ inches; back diagonal, $3\frac{1}{4}$ inches; edge, 41 inches; crown, from front to back, $14\frac{1}{2}$ inches, and from side to side, $13\frac{1}{4}$ inches.

32. Material Requirements.—For the covering, the materials required are $\frac{3}{8}$ yard of 40-inch-wide duvetyn and $\frac{1}{4}$ yard of 36-inch-wide gros de Londres. To trim the hat, $1\frac{1}{4}$ yards of No. 7 ribbon is needed.

33. Fitting the Brim.—Although the brim of this shape has a mushroom droop, the material can be fitted on it without a seam at the back. Therefore, lay the duvetyn over the top of the brim, one corner in the direct front, pin it on the edge at the front, the back, and the sides, and cut the material around the edge, allowing about $\frac{3}{4}$ inch as a margin. Next, cut the head-size opening, allowing $\frac{3}{4}$ inch to be slashed into tabs; then draw it down to the brim and stitch to the head-size band with a long-and-short basting-stitch.

Remove the pins around the outer edge, smooth and stretch the duvetyn out to the edge, gently working all the fulness out on the bias corners, and pin. For a smooth finish, apply a small quantity of millinery glue, spreading it evenly with a curling knife; then smooth and stretch the duvetyn out to the edge. Again trim the edge of the duvetyn, allowing about $\frac{1}{2}$ inch for a seam or margin, turn this over the edge of the brim, and stitch to the under brim with a small, slanting stitch, as shown in Fig. 41 and described in Art. **63,** *Elements of Millinery.*

For the under facing apply the duvetyn in the same manner. Lay a corner at the direct front, the back, and the sides. Cut the head-size opening and stitch to the head-size band, apply the glue, smooth and stretch the duvetyn out to the edge and trim the outer edge so that it has an even $\frac{1}{2}$-inch margin.

Next, measure off a piece of wire the exact circumference of the edge of the frame and join the ends with a clip. Beginning at the center back, turn the duvetyn over the wire so that it is even with the edge of the brim, and proceed to make a French finish, as described in Art. **67,** *Elements of Millinery.*

34. Making the Sectional Crown.—To develop a pattern for the six-piece sectional crown, divide the oval foundation crown into four parts by drawing a line from front to back and from side to side. Lay a piece of tissue paper over one of these sections and cut along the pencil mark. With this as a pattern, cut six pieces of material. Since the crown in the model is somewhat larger and softer than the foundation, the two extra sections will provide sufficient fulness in the crown.

Cover a No. 1 cable cord with duvetyn, making a loose-edge cord. Outline two of the sections with this cord; then attach another section on each side of these two, and, along the two uncorded edges of one set, attach the cord continuously, as shown at *a*, Fig. 12. Next, join the two sets of sections, pinning them on the wrong side at the center top first and then along one side. Turn the crown right side out to be sure that the intersection of the cords is in the exact center top, as at *b*. Continue pinning the sections together on the wrong side, as shown in Fig. 13, and then stitch together along the row of pins.

Now, turn right side out, draw the sectional crown down over the foundation crown, which has already been attached to the brim, and stitch around the base.

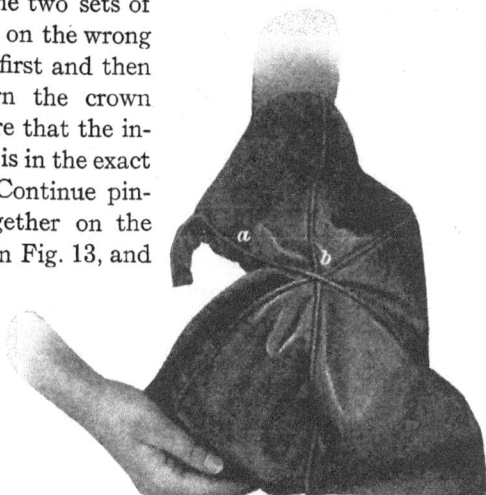

Fig. 12

Be sure that the cord dividing the two halves runs in a direct line from front to back. Adjust the sections and tack them at intervals to the foundation so as to give the easy effect shown.

35. Trimming.—A band of novelty ribbon drawn around the base and finished with a bow at the right side furnishes the only trimming in the model featured, but for a more dressy effect a spray of burnt peacock or a large-size, hand-made flower may be added. Or, other handwork, such as a design embroidered in each section or a wreath effect applied on the top brim may be used.

Fig. 13

SEMITRANSPARENT SUMMER MODEL

36. Nature of Model.—A hat to be worn with dainty frocks in summer is the semitransparent model shown in Fig. 14. It is developed in haircloth and French crêpe, requiring 1 yard of each. The foundation brim is made of wire according to the dimensions of the preceding model. Eight regulation support wires and a steel edge wire are used, but no round brace wires. The crown is a light-weight, oval shape molded in crinoline.

37. Covering the Brim.—After completing the wire foundation brim, wind the steel edge wire with maline, cover the under brim with haircloth, drawing the outer edge of the haircloth over the edge of the frame and in about 1 inch on top. Because this material is of a wiry nature and because no covering is used on the frame, one or two rows of running-stitches made of silk floss are used as a finish around the edge just inside the edge wire.

An extra extension brim of French crêpe projects about 2 inches over the edge of the horsehair brim. To make this brim, lay the hat brim on two thicknesses of French crêpe and cut the crêpe about 3 inches larger. Have each of the circles hemstitched about ½ inch from the edge and then cut them for a picot edge. Next, lay these circles over the top of the brim, pin to the edge in the direct front, the back, and the sides, cut the head-size opening, draw it down to the brim, and stitch to the head-size band.

FIG. 14

38. Covering the Crown.—To make the semisoft crown, cut a circle of the haircloth, about 9 inches, in diameter and run a shirr string around the edge. Lay this over the top of the crinoline foundation crown, pinning it at the front, the back, and the sides. Draw up the shirr string to fit the side crown, distribute the fulness evenly around, and sew to the side crown along the row of shirring. Because of the nature of the material, the top edge forms an easy, round, puff effect.

For the side crown, cut a bias strip of the haircloth 5 inches wide through the bias and long enough to reach around the crown.   In applying this side crown, do not stretch the haircloth; rather, lay it "easy" and make, by means of machine stitching, a straight or bias seam, whichever the material allows.   Then slip the side crown down over the foundation, turn it under at the base, and stitch it secure on the inside.   Next, cut a strip of brace wire the exact measurement of the top of the side crown at the place where the tip is sewed to the foundation, and join the ends with a clip.   Turn the top edge of the side-crown material over this wire and stitch with a row of back-stitches made of silk floss.

To give the soft, airy effect to the tip, cut away the foundation frame just above the rows of stitching at the top of the side crown. Then, attach the crown to the brim by stitching it on the inside; that is, taking the stitches in the foundation of the crown and around the top head-size wire.

39.   Trimming.—As a garniture for this style of hat, a spray of roses with rather long stems and dangling buds, laid across the front and extending beyond the edge on one side, forms a decidedly smart trim.

FIG. 15

FLAT, OR STRAIGHT-BRIM, BODY HAT

LEGHORN FLAT

40.   The straight brim of even dimensions, or the one-piece body hat, commonly called a *flat*, is perhaps the oldest type of head-gear considered appropriate for the growing girl after her soft-bonnet days have passed. Leghorn and fancy straw, for summer wear, and beaver and felt flats for winter wear, have been used continuously for children.

41.   Nature of Hat.—The hat shown in Fig. 15 is one type of leghorn flat.   It is woven in one piece; that is, the 5-inch brim is a continuation of the crown, which is a true oval shape about 4 inches high.

42.   Trimming.—Girlish simplicity is the keynote in the trimming arrangement, which is a band of No. 12 grosgrain ribbon drawn around the crown to the right-side back and finished with a two-end bow appliquéd flat to the side crown.   Extending out on the brim from under the cross-knot, two medium-sized, flat loops and two waist-length streamers complete this version of the flat family.

This style of trim requires 3½ yards of ribbon.

LEGHORN DRESS MODEL

43.   Nature of Hat.—The hat shown in Fig. 16 is the same as the one shown in Fig. 15, except that it is wired and developed into a midsummer, dress hat.   For this departure, the first step is to relieve the flexible appearance of the brim by wiring the edge with No. 21 brace wire and binding it with No. 3 moiré ribbon.   To soften the rather severe line, which this type of brim finish produces, side-plaited Val lace about 1 inch wide is used.

44.   Material Requirements.—If you desire the hat just as illustrated, provide, besides the leghorn, a 12-yard piece of Val lace, 1¼ yards of No. 3 moiré, 1⅛ yards of No. 100 moiré ribbon, and 1 bunch of morning glories.

FIG. 16

45.   Applying the Lace.—In applying the lace to the leghorn brim, extreme care must be exercised so as not to allow the stitches to show on the under brim.   Use a No. 9 millinery needle and No. 60 cotton thread for this work.   Draw up the coarse thread along the selvage of lace so as to allow the lace to lie flat and sew through this edge, slipping the needle each time under a strand of the leghorn, preferably along the ridge or cord.   Occasionally you may draw the needle through on the under facing, but in pushing it up again be sure to slip it under a strand of the braid.

Sew the first row of lace on the top brim so that the outer edge is just even with the edge of the brim.   Sew another row of the lace inside of this first row, overlapping the inner edge of the first row. Continue applying rows of lace in this way until you reach the head-size.

The entire crown, also, is covered with similar rows of lace. Beginning at the center back, apply the first row so that it just reaches the brim. When the center back is reached, instead of continuing spirally, cut and lap the lace. Then, the width of the lace above, apply the next row, and cut and lap at the back. Continue in this manner until the entire crown is covered. Because the lace is side-plaited, the joining of each row can easily be hidden by tacking the lap from the under side in a plait.

46. Trimming.—The added touch to this already charming hat is the generous-sized bunch of tiny, variegated morning glories applied to the brim on the left side, where the weight of the flowers dents the brim into a graceful droop. To balance this side trim, a band of colored No. 100 moiré ribbon is attached under the flowers and drawn across the front and over the edge to the under brim on the right side, where it is finished with a crushed loop, a knot, and a long shoulder streamer.

While this type of trimming is charming, it is not the only style of trim that is suitable for this type of hat. For instance, a wreath of various kinds of flowers applied tight around the base of the crown would be equally effective. The trimming arrangement, of course, should be governed by the personality of the wearer.

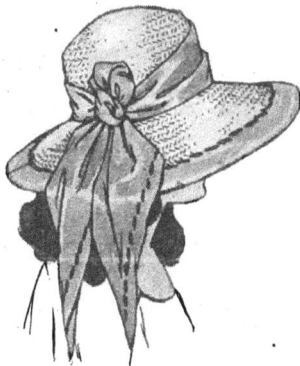

Fig. 17

REMODELED LEGHORN SPORTS HAT

47. Because of the extreme popularity of the leghorn hat, it returns each season, probably in a new style and shape, but always with marked regularity. Also, because of the durable wearing quality of this straw, one leghorn will, with a reasonable amount of care, last several years. Of course, in almost all cases, these leghorns will require touching up in order to be strictly up to date, but this is usually a simple matter.

48. Nature of Hat.—The hat shown in Fig. 17 is a child-size leghorn flat made into a suitable sports hat for a miss, by enlarging the brim about 1½ inches and adding a crêpe scarf. For this remodeling, 1 yard of 40-inch Georgette crêpe and some buckram are needed.

49. Altering the Brim.—To enlarge the brim, use buckram as the foundation and apply it in small pieces to the under brim, as in Fig. 18, lapping them slightly and sewing them to the edge of the brim by means of back-stitches, as shown at *a*, Fig. 18. After the buckram is sewed around the entire edge, with the measuring guide mark off 1¼ inches from the inside edge, as shown at *b*. Make the

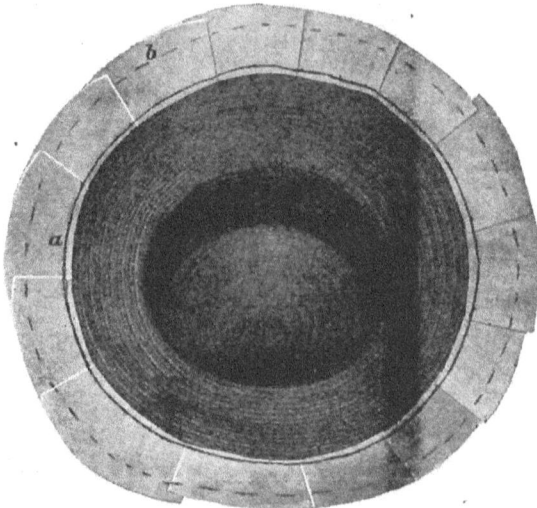

Fig. 18

line continuous all around the edge and cut. When cutting this edge, exercise care that you make it perfectly even, because the slightest niche will mar the finished edge.

If the brim has a tendency to droop more than is desired, attach the edge wire on the top of the brim on the extreme edge, but if the brim is inclined to ripple, then apply the wire on the under brim at the extreme edge. Next, bind the edge with a bias of crinoline.

50. Binding the Brim.—The outer binding on this model is of Georgette crêpe, but as this is transparent, it will be necessary to apply at first a binding of light-weight silk or silk-warp crêpe in order that the buckram will not show through. Because Georgette crêpe stretches much more than do other fabrics, when measuring for the binding, allow twice the width. Therefore, cut a bias strip of Georgette 12 inches wide through the bias, fold it in half to obtain two thicknesses, and draw it around the edge, pinning it in place. Cut off the bias corners and make a straight seam by machine-stitching it. Slip it over the edge again, turn in the raw edge, and baste it in an even line on top and underneath.

This binding may be turned over a wire and French-finished, but for a smart touch of hand-work that adds so much to sports hats, an overcast, or slanting-stitch, as shown, made with yarn in the same or in a contrasting color, is used. Apply this stitch so that it catches both top and underneath edges of the binding at the same time. After completing the stitching, you may remove the basting-stitches.

51. Scarf Trimming.—The simple scarf arrangement, also, is made of the Georgette. On a bias strip, 12 inches wide, run a ½-inch rolled hem on both sides, and on the bias ends run a 1-inch hem with yarn, as shown. · Also, on each of the pointed ends, you might embroider with the yarn a rose spray so as to give a decorative touch to an otherwise plain scarf.

After the ends are finished, draw the scarf around the crown to the right side and tie it in a bow [having one short loop and two ends.

RENOVATED SEMIDRESS LEGHORN

52. Nature of Hat.—The model shown in Fig. 19 is another suggestion for utilizing a past-season, leghorn flat with a small crown, or one that has become burnt or faded

FIG. 19

with the sun. Or, this form of remodeling may be applied to any other type of body hat, such as beavers, felts, or fancy braids.

To put into effect this method of remodeling on a medium-sized leghorn, 1 yard of 27-inch silk is sufficient.

53. Remodeling the Brim.—To alter the brim, cut off the crown about ¾ inch above the regular head-size. If the head-size opening is too small, slash tabs as far as the width of one braid on the brim, shape them up with the thumb for the new head-size, and along this line, on the top of the brim, attach a narrow ribbon wire to support the head-size. Next, apply the top facing of silk out to about 1½ inches from the edge and finish it with a cord by means of a French finish, as shown.

54. Making the Crown.—Procure a regulation, oval, foundation crown of netine and cover it plain with the silk, drawing the fulness down at the diagonal points. Then, for the cuff effect, join in a ring a bias strip of crinoline 5 inches wide through the bias and long enough to reach around the base of the crown. Next, turn down about 1 inch of this strip along the top edge and shape it out until it measures 1 inch more in circumference than along the other edge.

Fig. 20

Now, cover this cuff with a bias piece of the silk. In applying the silk, endeavor not to stretch or draw the cuff out of shape; rather, lay the silk around in a firm, but easy, manner, make a machine-stitched seam at the back, turn down the top edge, and catch it to the inside of the cuff. Next, slip the cuff down over the crown and stitch it to the base of the crown. Turn the lower edge of the silk over the base and stitch it to the inside of the foundation crown. With the entire crown ready, attach it to the brim by stitching firmly from the inside.

55. Trimming.—Now apply the trimming, which in this case is a spray of fruits and flowers at the right-side front. Any other type of trimming preferred, however, may be substituted.

FANCY-STRAW, FLOPPY-BRIM FLAT

56. The hat shown in Fig. 20 is a regulation flat of novelty, or fancy, straw. A wreath of long-stemmed field flowers encircles the base of the crown and extends out on the brim in simple, youthful fashion. When this hat is placed on the head, the natural suppleness of the brim causes it to droop in an easy, graceful manner. Owing to this feature, this type of hat is called a floppy-brim hat.

FABRIC, FLOPPY-BRIM FLAT

57. Nature of Hat.—Another innovation of the floppy-brim type, but one developed in a fabric, is shown in Fig. 21. This generous-sized, dressy hat intended for the young girl's "Sunday best" is made of 1 yard of 36-inch navy faille and trimmed with a spray of hand-made wool flowers. While any other material or all-over straw fabric may be used in constructing this model, the selection of silk makes it suitable for all-year wear.

58. Suitable Frame.—For this model, a straight, sailor frame of the following dimensions is necessary: Head-size, 23 inches; width of brim, $3\frac{1}{4}$ inches; edge, $43\frac{1}{2}$ inches. This frame may be of netine, buckram, or wire. If a wire frame is used, the under brim must be covered with one layer of crinoline before the silk is applied.

Fig. 21

59. Making the Brim.—To make this soft, floppy, or cushion-brim, effect, lay the silk over the top brim, as described for fitting a brim plain, and pin it at the front, the back, and the sides. Cut the silk about 2 inches larger than the founda-

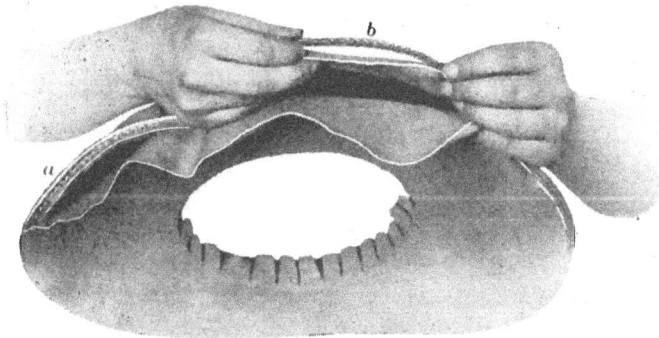

Fig. 22

tion frame, slash the head-size opening, draw the silk down to the head-size, and stitch secure. Next, smooth and stretch the silk out to the edge and pin. With the measuring guide, measure a distance of 1½ inches larger than the frame edge and cut the edge of the silk perfectly even.

Next, cut the under facing in the same manner as described for the top, slash the head-size, and stitch to the head-size band, smoothing and stretching the silk out to the edge. Apply a small quantity of millinery glue on the under brim to hold the silk facing to it. Next, trim the outer edge so that this facing is the same size as the top facing

60. Applying the Cord Finish.—Make a loose-edge cord with a No. 1 cable cord and attach it around the edge of the silk on the top facing, as shown at *a*, Fig. 22. A portion of the cord, while it is being applied to the edge, is shown at *b*, and the part shown at *c*

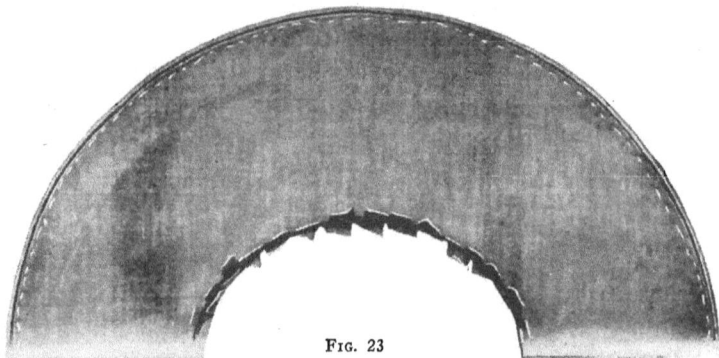

Fig. 23

illustrates the manner in which the underfacing is turned under to meet the cord. After you have sewed the cord around the edge, trim off the raw edges as close to the row of stitching as possible to avoid a thick or lumpy edge; then turn the raw edges back and baste around the edge, as shown in Fig. 23.

Next, smooth and adjust the under facing, trim off the edge, if necessary, to make it even, turn this edge in until it just meets the cord, and baste in place, as shown in Fig. 24. Then slip-stitch this edge to the cord, exercising care that the edge is turned in perfectly even before you begin to slip-stitch it.

In doing the slip-stitching, take the stitches very close together along the row of stitching that is used to join the cord to the upper brim. Remove the basting, and the brim, which has a 1-inch extension forming a flexible edge, is complete.

61. Making the Crown.—For the two-piece, semisoft crown, draw a bias strip of netine, 3 inches wide, around the head-size of the brim, lap it 1 inch at the back, and wire with brace wire on the inside of the top edge. Shirr around the edge a circle of faille 13

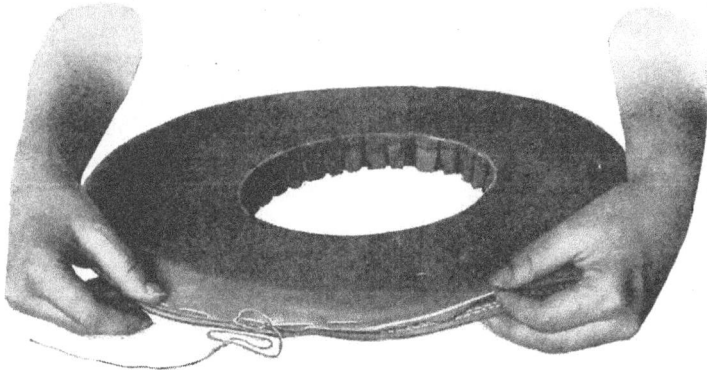

Fig. 24

inches in diameter, running one row of shirring on the extreme edge and another 1 inch from this. Slip this tip over the top edge of the netine side crown, distribute the fulness evenly around, and stitch along the first row of shirring. Next, apply the plain-fitted side crown according to the method given in Art. **38,** for semi-transparent model.

62. Trimming.—After the crown is attached to the brim, apply a spray of hand-made yarn flowers, as shown, or any other appropriate trimming, and dent the edge of the foundation brim, if a decidedly floppy effect is desired.

STRAIGHT-BRIM, VAL-LACE MODEL

63. Nature of Hat.—The effectiveness of Val lace for an entire hat is demonstrated to a marked degree in the fetching, straight-brimmed model illustrated in Fig. 25. A hat of this

Fig. 25

kind is especially appropriate for wear with dainty, summer frocks.

64. Materials Required.—In order that this hat may assume a transparent effect, you will need a wire foundation brim whose dimensions are: Head-size, 23 inches; width of brim, $3\frac{1}{2}$ inches; and length of edge wire, which is steel, $43\frac{1}{2}$ inches.

For the molded crown and to cover the wire brim, you will need 2 yards of maline. To develop the hat, 20 yards of Val lace is needed, and, for trimming, $1\frac{1}{2}$ yards of ribbon.

65. Making the Brim.—The first step in the making of the brim is to wind the edge wire with 2-inch-wide strips of white maline until it presents an even, round finish. Then, with the maline folded as it comes from the bolt, or in two thicknesses, double it over the edge wire. Securing it firmly with pins at the

Fig. 26

center back, draw it firmly around the edge, but do not stretch it as in the case of covering other transparent brims. Next, stitch it to the edge wire on the top by means of a row of fine running-stitches, draw the top portion into the head size band, and stitch. Allow the under facing to be free until the Val lace is applied, and then draw it in to the head-size and stitch to the head-size wire.

66. Applying the Lace.—As you apply the lace, draw up the coarse thread on the inner edge at intervals of about $\frac{1}{2}$ yard in order to give an easy frill to it, tie the threads, and clip them close. Beginning at the center back, attach the first row on the edge wire, allowing it to extend the full width of the lace. Continue it spirally into the head-size on the top brim, sewing each row so that the outer edge just laps the inner, or sewed, edge of the preceding row.

67. Making the Crown.—For the transparent crown, shape four thicknesses of maline down over an oval, buckram, foundation crown, pinning it around the head-size. Beginning at the base in the center back, apply the Val lace, sewing it flat and just through the maline. Take the stitches on the scalloped edge of the lace, as shown in Fig. 26, but of course take them smaller than those illustrated, these being put in with black thread and made somewhat large in order that they may easily be observed. Continue sewing the lace spirally to the top of the side crown; then, to make it conform to the outline of the crown, draw up a trifle the coarse thread in the plain edge. Continue the sewing as for the side crown until the center is reached, then make a neat, flat finish at this point.

Before removing the buckram foundation, hold the crown over a steaming teakettle and allow the steam to penetrate every part of it. Next, remove the pins around the base, slip the buckram foundation out, cut away the extra maline around the base, and attach the finished crown to the brim, sewing it securely to the head-size band.

68. Making the Collar.—To make the extra collar that serves as part of the trimming, fold a piece of maline half the usual width and 24 inches long into four thicknesses, making a strip 3 inches wide. Stretch and curve the doubled edge until it measures 1 inch more than the other edge. About ½ inch from the top, or curved, edge, sew a row of Val lace slightly frilled; below this row, or the width of the lace apart, apply two other rows. Then, ½ inch below the last row, cut away any extra maline and apply the collar around the base of the crown, applying it at the right-side back, or under the point where the trimming is to be applied.

69. Trimming.—To complete the hat, a wee band of tinseled blue ribbon is drawn around the base of the crown to hide the joining of the collar to the brim, and a trailing bunch of dainty flowers, in which several loops of the ribbon are entwined, is applied at the right-side back.

BRETON SAILOR

70. Nature of Hat.—In Fig. 27 is shown a transparent, hair-braid model developed over a Breton-sailor shape, which takes its name from the native head-gear of Brittany. As will be noted, it has an easy-rolling brim which droops a little at the head-size and then rolls upward. A $2\frac{1}{2}$-inch lacy hair braid makes the brim and a 1-inch hair braid is used for the crown. The hat of itself is sufficiently dressy to require no trimming except a profusion of ribbon loops and ends that fall from the center back over the brim.

71. Foundation Frame. This model is developed over a wire brim made according to the outline of the foundation frame shown in Fig. 28, and having dimensions as follows: Head-size, 23 inches; width of brim, $3\frac{1}{2}$ inches; edge wire, 44 inches; oval crown, back to front, 15 inches;

Fig. 27

Fig. 28

and side to side, 14 inches. After making a wire brim according to these brim dimensions, apply an extra round brace wire through

the center of the brim in order to define the roll.   It is not necessary to make a wire mold for the crown, as this may be developed
over the buckram crown and then removed from it.

72. Materials Required.—The materials required for this
model are a 5-yard piece of 2½-inch lacy hair braid for the brim,
6 yards of 1-inch hair braid for the crown, and 3 yards each of the
five different-colored ribbons.

73. Tinting and Winding the Brim Wires.—Whether the brim
wires are tinted and wound depends on the color chosen for the hat.
If it is made in black, which is a good selection for a miss in her
teens, black wire should be used for the brim, and then no tinting
will be necessary.   But if one of the pretty, pastel colors is chosen,
it will be found advisable to make the frame for the brim out of
white wire and then tint it the same color as the braid.   Also, for
either black or colors, the edge and the round brace wire should be
wound with maline in a matching color so that it will not be difficult
to conceal the stitches used in applying the braid to the brim.

74. Covering the Brim With Maline.—Before the hair braid is
applied to the brim, it must first be covered with maline.   To do
this, take the maline as it comes from the bolt, or in two thicknesses,
and double it over the edge wire.   Beginning at the back, draw it
firmly around the edge, stretching it as much as possible all the
way around.   Pin it at intervals inside the edge wire and lap it
about 3 inches at the back, making it secure with a stitch or with
pins.   Then, draw all the fulness into the head-size and pin it
securely.

Next, hold the covered brim over a steaming kettle and, while
doing so, draw the maline until all the fulness is drawn in at the head-
size.   To make the top portion of the maline conform to the shape
of the brim, run a row of fine stitches along the round brace wire;
then sew both facings together with a row of running-stitches inside
the head-size wire.

75. Applying the Hair Braid to the Brim.—Only the under brim
of this model is covered with braid, two rows of 2½-inch braid being
sufficient.   With a very fine stitch, sew the first row of lacy hair
braid to the maline-wound edge wire so that it extends about ½ inch
beyond the edge of the frame.   This will make the brim about
2 inches larger in circumference than the frame shown in Fig. 27.

Lap the braid about 1 inch at the back and tack the inner edge to the round brace wire. Lap the next row of braid about $\frac{1}{2}$ inch over the first row, stitch on the outer edge of the braid along the round brace wire, and, on the inner edge, around the head-size wire.

76. Making the Crown.—The crown of this model is made of hair braid, but of an even, plain weave, in a narrow width. For the transparent effect, shape a layer of fine tarlatan down over the oval buckram foundation and pin it around the head-size.

Beginning at the base in the center back, apply the braid, sewing it just through the tarlatan. Continue sewing it spirally until the

Fig. 29

center top is reached and make a neat, flat finish at this point. Hold the finished crown over a steaming kettle and allow the steam to penetrate every part of the crown. Remove the pins around the base, slip the buckram foundation out, and the transparent crown will appear as shown in Fig. 29. Next, cut away the extra tarlatan around the base and attach the crown to the brim, sewing it securely to the head-size band.

77. Trimming.—To complete the hat, draw bands of several different colors of narrow, picoted ribbon around the side crown to the center back, and let them fall in a veritable shower of loops and ends from this point out over the brim. However, the type of trimming and its arrangement will depend largely on the fashion prevailing when the hat is made.

VARIATION OF BRETON SHAPE

78. Nature of Hat.—In the model illustrated in Fig. 30, the foundation frame shown in Fig. 28 is again employed, but a solid fabric is chosen; also, the width of the brim is broken by the material being applied plain on a portion of it and soft around the edge. These features make the hat particularly appropriate for the girl with a long, thin face, as such a type requires softness of brim line; while the plump, round-face girl looks better in a rather plain, severe brim, such as is shown in Fig. 28. For this hat, the brim is made to assume a broad, off-the-face shape by grasping it on the direct sides and denting or shaping the edge wire down.

79. Material Requirements.—The material to be employed may be allover fabric, such as velvet, silk, duvetyn, straw cloth, or braid. In this case, 18-inch velvet is used, 1½ yards being sufficient. For the trimming, 1¼ yards of ribbon is required.

80. Making the Plain-Fitted Under Facing.—Apply the plain-fitted portion of the under facing first according to the method already given; that is, lay the material over the under brim with the corner in the direct front, and pin it about 1 inch in from the edge and at the head-size, shaping and smoothing it to

Fig. 30

conform to the line of the brim, then cut away the surplus velvet just outside of the pins. Slash around the head-size, sew to the head-size band, and slip-stitch the seam at the back. Next, smooth and stretch the facing out to the edge and stitch.

81. Making the Soft Extension and Top Facing.—For the soft-edge effect, which is a continuation of the top brim, cut two bias strips of velvet 8 inches wide through the bias and 18 inches long, and join them in a ring. Then divide into four equal parts by making a cross with two pins for the center front and the center back and using the seams for the direct sides. Next, run a shirr string along one edge.

On the under facing, about ½ inch inside the edge of the under brim, apply the shirred edge, pinning it at the front, the back, and the sides, and draw up the shirr string. Distribute the fulness with the needle point, pushing it around to the direct sides, as shown, so as to give a rather broad effect to the hat, and sew secure.

Next, run three rows of shirring about 1 inch apart along the other edge of the velvet and draw this edge into the head-size on top, allowing it to form a soft, easy roll over the edge, as shown.

82. Making the Crown.—For the crown, lay a 15-inch square of velvet over the top, and draw it down to the head-size in a row of even, small-sized plaits. Sew the velvet to the head-size, and, if a soft crown is desired, cut away the foundation about 1 inch from the head-size. The regulation cap lining will give sufficient support. With the crown made, sew it securely to the brim.

83. Trimming.—As a garniture, appliqué a spray of vari-colored flowers across the front and draw a band of narrow ribbon around the base of the crown, finishing it in a tiny tie-bow at the direct back.

BOLERO, OR CHIN-CHIN, TURBAN

FOUNDATION FRAME

84. Nature of Frame.—When the Breton brim assumes a deeper and closer roll toward the crown, it becomes a replica of the hat worn by a Spanish dancer and is called a *bolero, chin-chin,* or *cuff turban.* The frame shown in Fig. 31 is a junior edition of the bolero, or cuff, turban, having a ready-made oval crown and flexible brim of netine. Like the poke and sailor shapes, this type of hat, with various modifications, occupies a very important position in hatdom for juveniles.

85. Versatility of Frame.—Numerous designs may be obtained by using this frame as a foundation, such as fitting the brim perfectly plain with any of the season's popular fabrics and decorating the brim with embroidery or fancy stitches. Also, it serves as an excellent block for developing frameless hats; that is, hats made of ribbon, straw braid, or bias folds. These materials may be shaped over this frame during the sewing processes, after which the frame can be removed and the material will retain the shape.

86. Making the Cuff Brim.—To develop the cuff brim illustrated, make a 22-inch, head-size band of No. 7 ribbon wire, and to it apply a bias strip of netine 5 inches through the bias and 10 inches longer than the circumference of the head-size band. Because netine is pliable, it can easily be shaped into the head-size without any fulness and made to assume an easy roll at the head-size as well

Fig. 31

as a considerable variety of brim styles that are easy to wear.

After the netine is shaped into the head-size, lap it 1 inch at the back, and trim off the edge evenly, or until it measures $3\frac{1}{4}$ inches all around. Apply a No. 21 brace wire on the outside edge, as shown in Fig. 31, stretching the edge as the wire is being attached until it measures 31 inches in circumference. Before applying the material, bind this wire with a bias strip of crinoline.

Fig. 32

WINTER MODEL

87. Material Requirements.—The hat shown in Fig. 32 is developed on the cuff-brim shape just described. Velvet is used for this model, but any other fabric, such as duvetyn, silk, or material matching the child's coat, may be substituted. To copy the model exactly, provide $1\frac{1}{4}$ yards of 18-inch velvet and 7 yards or rope chenille.

88. Cutting Material For Brim.—As the material for the brim is applied softly and extends about 1 inch higher than the foundation frame, to allow for this extension and soft effect, it will be necessary to cut the material wider and longer than the measurement of the frame. Therefore, for the brim, cut a bias strip of velvet 37 inches long and 10 inches wide and join the ends in a ring.

89. Smocking.—Since the circumference of the edge is greater than that around the head-size, to take care of this fulness and also to add a touch of novel hand-work, the velvet is stitched at intervals from nearly the edge of the brim to the head-size to give the effect of smocking. Like real smocking, the stitches are made on the back, or wrong side, of the material. To do this work, the material should be blocked off; however, by using the small measuring guide, this work can be done rapidly and without any difficulty.

Considering the width of the brim, which is $3\frac{1}{4}$ inches, and allowing for a $\frac{3}{4}$-inch seam at the head-size, measure a distance of 4 inches from one edge of the material and mark with a pin. Without removing the measure, put in another pin at the 3-inch mark and another at the 2-inch mark. Then, 1 inch from these markings, fold the material in the same manner. At a distance of $3\frac{1}{2}$ inches from the edge, insert a pin, and again, at $2\frac{1}{2}$ inches, at $1\frac{1}{2}$ inches, and at $\frac{1}{2}$ inch from the edge.

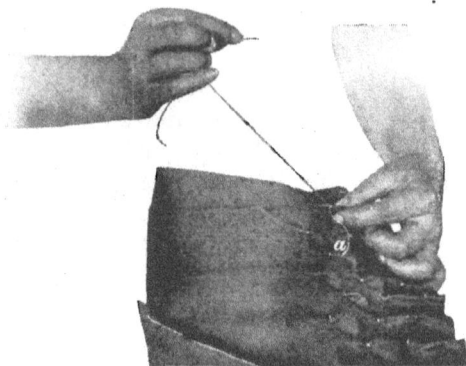

FIG. 33

At the points indicated by the pins, take a stitch about $\frac{1}{4}$ inch deep and draw the thread up to about 3 inches from the end, allowing this end to hang free, as shown at a, Fig. 33. Take two or three firm overcast-stitches, always inserting the needle in the same holes; then with the free end make a tie-stitch, as shown in Fig. 34, and clip the ends close to the knot. Apply similar stitches at the points where the pins are placed. In this way, continue marking and stitching two rows at a time around the entire piece of material used for the brim.

90. Applying the Material to the Brim.—When the smocking is complete, run a shirr string along both edges and lay the material over the brim with the smocked portion coming on the under brim of the frame.   Pin it around the edge and the head-size and shape it to conform to the outline of the frame.   Before drawing the top facing into the head-size, make a row of invisible stitches around the edge, which will catch the outer row of smocking-stitches to the edge of the brim.   Then draw the top facing into the head-size, allowing the folded edge to extend in a soft effect, and stitch.

91.   Making the Crown.—The crown of this hat is made in two pieces and is just large enough to allow the hat to fit well down on

Fig. 34

the head.   A circle 6½ inches in diameter is used for the tip, and a bias strip 21 inches long and 5 inches wide, joined in a ring, for the side crown.

Join the side crown to the tip by machine-stitching a seam around the edge of the circle; turn it right side out and apply it to the brim without the foundation crown, slip-stitching it securely to the velvet on the top brim.   A cap lining made in the same manner will give sufficient support to this crown.

92.   Trimming.—At the right side, a tassel effect is produced by looping several strands of chenille and attaching them to the edge of the brim at the right side.   Another style of trimming that is appropriate for this type of hat consists of an embroidered band placed around the top of the side crown and finished with a tassel.

93.   Nature of Hat.—The hat shown in Fig. 35 is another model developed on the foundation frame shown in Fig. 30.   It

is made of a combination of fabric and straw braid in one color or a combination of colors.   For such a model, the materials required are one 10-yard piece of maline braid and $\frac{1}{2}$ yard of 36-inch silk.

94.   Covering the Brim.—For the first step, cover the foundation brim with a bias strip of silk cut long enough to reach around the edge and wide enough to reach from the head-size on top over the edge to the head-size underneath.

Fig. 35

95.   Making the Wheels.—For the wheels, cut twelve circular pieces of crinoline $2\frac{1}{2}$ inches in diameter. Next, fold $1\frac{1}{2}$-inch-wide maline braid in half and run a shirr string along the double edge.   To apply the braid to the disks, begin at the outer edge and sew the braid along the shirr string, shaping it to form a roll, as shown at a, Fig. 36.

So as to graduate the braid for a neat finish in the center, about 3 inches from the end run the shirr string in a long bias line, as shown at b.   Next, cut off the double edge of the braid outside this bias line, draw up the shirr string enough to shape the braid into the center, push the end through a hole made in the center, and make a neat finish by fastening the end on the wrong side.

96.   Applying the Wheels.—Apply these disks around the outside of the cuff brim, al-

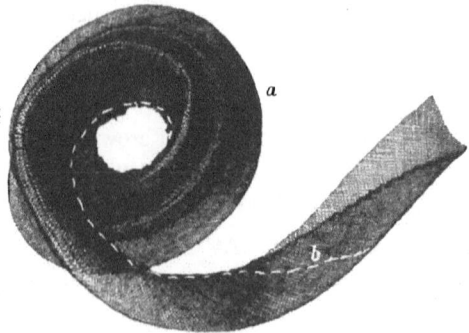

Fig. 36

lowing them to extend a little above the top edge and also to show the covering of the brim around the head-size.   Then draw out the brim and shape it down at the sides to give a broad, rather than a round, effect.

97. Covering the Crown.—If a two-tone effect is desired, cover the crown plain with the same kind of silk as was used for the brim. Then, beginning at the base, sew the braid spirally to the center top. Because the braid is transparent, the silk will show through and produce a two-tone effect or a combination of colors.

98. Completing the Hat.—Attach the crown to the brim and then draw around the side crown a band of silk in the same or a contrasting color, finishing it at the back with a flat tailored bow.

BLOCKED BOLERA

99. Nature of Shape.—The hat shown in Fig. 37 is a seven-end milan, blocked shape, with an usually smart tailleur trim of faille ribbon at the right side. The brim of this model might be termed a cross between a Breton and a bolero because of its being too small for a Breton and too low for a bolero. Also, instead of the regulation dome or oval crown that usually accompanies these brims, the crown in this model is a rather tall apex, thus showing how variable in contour these shapes can be.

Although this model is of the finest grade of milan, the same shape, for summer wear, comes in patent milan and numerous other straws that make very durable hats for

Fig. 37

school and knock-about wear. For winter, it may be had in scratch felt, beaver, and velours.

100. Trimming.—For the trim, you will need 2½ yards of No. 9 faille ribbon. First, draw a band around the crown to the right side. Next, to make the hoop effect, join two strips of No. 7 ribbon wire in a ring with a 1-inch lap, and twist the faille ribbon around these rings. Then attach the loops to the right side crown over the joining of the band. Wrap another strip of ribbon ¾ yard long over the joining and make a one-loop-and-two-end bow to extend just beyond the edge.

CLOCHE SHAPE

SPORTS MODEL

101. Nature of Hat.—Standing out prominently among the other shapes that are used for grown-ups and juveniles alike, is the cloche, one of which is shown in Fig. 38. This smart sports model is suitable for a girl of the sub-deb age. Baronet visca is the fabric selected for making the hat, and a bandanna handkerchief of gay coloring serves as an edge binding and scarf around the coronet.

102. Foundation Frame.—The frame shown in Fig. 39, a true cloche shape, is used for the foundation of this model. The dimensions of its brim are: Head-size, 24 inches; back, $1\frac{1}{2}$ inches; front, $1\frac{3}{4}$ inches; sides, $2\frac{1}{4}$ inches; front diagonal, $1\frac{3}{4}$ inches; back diagonal, $1\frac{3}{4}$ inches; and edge, 32 inches. Its crown measures, from back to front, 14 inches, and from side to side, 13 inches.

103. Covering the Brim.—Although the brim has a decided droop or bowl shape, the visca allover is pliable enough to be stretched over it without a seam. Lay the material over the top brim according to the method already given. Since the edge is bound with another fabric, it is not necessary to allow the extra margin; therefore, cut the material close to the edge and stitch with a firm back-stitch. Cover the under brim next, using a little millinery glue in order to make the visca conform to the shape of the brim, and back-stitch around the edge.

FIG. 38

104. Covering the Crown.—To cover the crown, draw a square of the visca down over the oval foundation, working the fulness out at the diagonal points. Cover the coronet with a bias strip of the visca, shaping it into the folds. Next, slip the coronet down over the crown and stitch around the base, turning the bottom edge of the coronet covering over the base of the crown and stitching to the inside of the foundation crown.

105. Preparing and Applying the Binding.—Before attaching the crown to the brim, make and apply the edge binding. For the binding and scarf effect, cut a 24-inch square bandanna handkerchief diagonally through the center. From one corner, cut a bias strip 3 inches wide, for the binding. Stretch this strip around the edge of the brim to determine the length required; cut off this length, allowing $\frac{1}{2}$ inch for a straight seam; then machine-stitch the seam and press it flat. Now, turn both edges inward until they meet in the center and sew them loosely with a catch-stitch. Be very careful not to make this stitching too tight, or when the binding is put on the edge it will pucker.

After the binding is prepared, stretch it around the edge, exercising care so as not to stretch the under portion and making sure that it is the same width on the top and on the under brim. Next, sew the binding by means of slip-stitching; that

Fig. 39

is, slip-stitch the turned-under edge of the binding to the covering of the top brim, and then, reversing the hat, slip-stitch the turned-under edge on the under facing.

106. Completing the Hat.—Now attach the crown to the brim. Then, on the raw edge of the remaining portion of the bandanna handkerchief, make a rolled hem and drape the corner around the coronet, having the point in the direct front. This point may be arranged so that it stands up in diadem fashion, or it may be tucked down over the cuff, the other two points being tied in a sailor's knot at the back.

The other corner of the handkerchief may be used as a neck scarf, as shown, thus completing a decidedly novel sports set.

Numerous other trimming arrangements can be used on this particular model such as a broad quill effect, fancy feathers, or any of the smart ribbon trims.

BROAD-OF-SIDES CLOCHE

107. Nature of Hat.—A modification of the cloche is shown in Fig. 40. The brim of this model, instead of drooping in close to the head, spreads out, giving a broad-of-sides line, which is enlarged also by the ruffles of Val lace extending out beyond the edge.

Developed in chiffon and Val lace in faint pastel tones for a dainty miss in her early teens, this hat breathes the very inspiration of summer. It carries out the idea of stretching the chiffon over an opaque foundation frame just as taffeta or a similar fabric is used. The beauty of the color effect cannot here be given, but the assembling of coral pink chiffon or Georgette crêpe over azure-blue is just what appeals to the growing girl. However, any other combination of colors may be substituted if the wearer so desires.

108. Material Requirements.—To produce the model as illustrated, the materials required are ¾ yard of two colors of chiffon or Georgette crêpe, 6 yards of lace, and 1¼ yards of ribbon.

109. Covering the Brim.—To cover the brim, lay two layers of azure-blue chiffon and one layer of pink over the top brim, and fit it according to the method given for Fig. 11. Use one layer of blue

Fig. 40

for the under facing, and finish it with a cord around the outer edge. If the material used is of a very thin quality, it may be necessary to use two thicknesses, but with a good grade of chiffon or Georgette crêpe, one is sufficient.

110. Adding the Lace.—Hand-tint the Val lace with some soap dye or powder to give a faint tone of pink. Draw up the thread in the plain edge to frill it and apply it in rows to the under facing, sewing it to the covering only. Apply the first row just inside the cord on the edge and allow it to extend its full width beyond the edge.

111. Making the Crown.—According to the method given for Fig. 6, make a soft crown in balloon fashion, with two layers of pink over one layer of blue chiffon. You may crush this crown down over an oval foundation, or for a decidedly, soft effect you may omit the foundation and supply a cap effect of the chiffon as a foundation.

112. Trimming.—As the finishing touch in daintiness and color appeal, draw a band of azure-blue picot ribbon around the base of the crown to the right-side back, where a spray of sunset roses falls off the brim.

ALL-YEAR CLOCHE MODEL

113. Nature of Hat.—Following the same line of brim and crown as in Fig. 39, but with the cuff omitted, the model shown in Fig. 41 is made still larger by the generous extension of the ribbon loops that are used to cover the top brim. This particular model offers many possibilities, because the ribbon arrangement gives an excellent idea for covering a medium-sized straw flat that has become faded or burnt with the sun. Also, the combination of ribbon with crêpe de Chine of the same or a contrasting color for an under facing, makes an especially pretty model for all-year wear.

FIG. 41

To develop it, 5 yards of No. 40 faille ribbon and ⅜ yard of crêpe de Chine are required.

114. Making the Brim.—To develop this model, cover the under brim first, bringing the covering about 1½ inches on the top brim, as described for Fig. 9. Then cut nine strips of No. 40 faille ribbon 7 inches long, for the brim loops. In one end of each of the strips run a shirr string.

Apply the center, or direct-front, strip first, and then apply the others, pinning the slightly shirred end of each one along the row of stitching on the top of the under facing, as shown in Fig. 42. Then sew them along the line of pins and turn them up to the side crown and pin, as shown in Fig. 43, forming 1½-inch extension loops around the edge of the brim and lapping the top edge of the loops to conform to the shape of the crown. Stitch along the line of pins and remove them.

115.   Making the Crown.—For the tip, cut eight strips of ribbon 6 inches long and miter one end of each about 2 inches.

Fig. 42

Join these eight pieces together as described for making sectional crowns, and apply the crown over the top of the oval foundation.

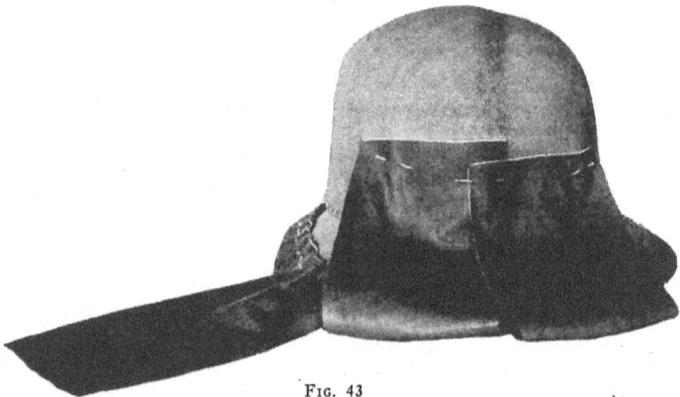

Fig. 43

To cover the joining of the brim loops and crown, draw a band of the ribbon, with the top edge turned down about $\frac{3}{4}$ inch, around to the right side.

116.   Trimming.—For a finish over this joining, attach a strip of the ribbon, 10 inches long, which has been fringed about 3 inches on one end. Turn the other end down at the top of the side-crown band and finish it at this point with four small, covered, button molds. Tack the strip with an invisible stitch at the base of the ribbon band, and allow the fringed end to extend out on the brim and over the edge.

This simple tailored trim may be elaborated on by several different-sized loops, or the side-crown band may be embroidered to produce a touch of brilliant color.

SUMMER MODEL

117. Nature of Hat.—Sweet simplicity is suggested in the quaint "youthified" version of the cloche shown in Fig. 44. This, too, is developed over an opaque foundation of netine and, although its lines are exactly the same as those of the model shown in Fig. 39 and are suitable for grown-up sister, its head-size is made to fit a maid of 5 or 6 summers. Also, it manages, through the designer's skill, to possess that air of childish simplicity so essential in hats for this youthful type.

118. Material Requirements.—Although made entirely of frilled Val lace, this hat, by means of its brim, provides an opportunity for the introduction of a touch of color in the material used to cover the frame before the lace is applied. When the right

Fig. 44

selection is made in this covering, which may be crêpe or light-weight silk, much expressiveness is given to the little tot. To develop this model, 18 yards of Val lace and ½ yard of crêpe or silk are needed.

119. Covering the Brim.—Cut a bias strip of the fabric, long enough to fit around the edge of the brim and wide enough from the head-size on top over the edge to the head-size underneath, and apply this over the foundation brim. Next apply the narrow Val lace, slightly frilled, on the top brim, the outer edge of the first row of lace being just even with the brim edge. Continue the lace spirally into the head-size, spacing the rows a little more than the width of the lace apart so that the color will show a little. Then apply it to the under facing in the same manner.

120. Covering the Crown.—First cover the oval-shaped foundation crown with the colored crêpe, and then apply the frilled Val lace spirally. Begin sewing the lace at the head-size and finish it neatly at the center top. Place the row around the head-size so that when the crown is attached to the brim, the line of demarcation will be barely visible.

121. Applying the Trimming.—Attach a bunch of vari-colored forget-me-nots so that they nestle close to the crown on the left side of the brim. This trimming forms the sole garniture of the hat, but it is one that never fails to appeal to the little tots.

WINTER MODEL

122. Nature of Hat.—Developed out of a fabric suitable for winter wear, the hat shown in Fig. 45 also uses the cloche foundation shown in Fig. 39. A variation is obtained, however, by applying the material on the brim so that it extends in a soft puff effect and thereby enlarges the brim several inches. For the crown, the material is side-plaited, the plaiting continuing the soft, full effect of the brim.

123. Material Requirements.—For this model, one material, such as silk, Canton crêpe, velvet, or duvetyn may be used, or two fabrics may be combined. A plan that is often followed is to make the brim out of material used in the coat and then use a contrasting fabric and color for the crown, or vice versa. Just as the hat is featured, it requires $1\frac{1}{8}$ yards of 18-inch chiffon velvet and 2 yards of ribbon.

FIG. 45

124. Estimating the Brim Material.—To copy the hat, make the brim in one-piece effect; that is, make the top and under brim out of the same piece. When estimating the amount required for this type of brim, allow one and one-half times the circumference of the edge, in some cases adding a few inches for an extra large extension. The circumference of this cloche shape is 32 inches, so one and one-half times this, or 48 inches, is the length of the piece required. An extra allowance is not needed for this brim, for, although the material extends beyond the edge, the 48 inches will be sufficient for fulness.

125. Making the Brim.—Cut two bias strips of 18-inch wide velvet, each 7 inches wide through the bias. Seam the two pieces and join the ends in a ring. Along each edge, run three rows of shirring ¾ inch apart. Lay the piece over the top brim, with the seams coming on each side, and draw up the first row of shirring to fit the head-size band. Distribute the fulness evenly all around and then draw the other two rows up in like manner. Arrange the shirring with the needle point and pin the material in place.

Next, draw the under facing into the head-size and draw up the shirr strings for the top. After pinning it in place around the head-size, take a row of invisible stitches along the outer row of shirring to hold the under facing in place. Next, sew the top and under facing around the head-size band.

126. Making the Crown.—For the crown, the velvet is side-plaited by machine. Join together two 18-inch bias strips of velvet, 7½ inches through the bias, and have this piece side-plaited. Cut off the two bias corners in a plait and make a straight seam. Lay this around the oval foundation crown, turn under at the head-size, and stitch on the inside. Next, run a shirr string along the top edge, draw it up tight, and finish with a flat, velvet-covered disk.

127. Trimming.—As a trim, draw a band of narrow ribbon around the crown. Apply a novelty flat bow of three 2-inch loops and three 2-inch ends at the front a little to the left and finish with a small floral medallion in the center.

As in the case of other models, this type affords many opportunities for variation in trimming.

TAMS

NATURE AND VARIETY OF TAMS

128. The tam, which is universally accepted as belonging to the youthful, is fashioned after the tight-fitting, woolen cap that forms a part of the regular Scottish costume. It consists of a tight-fitting head-band and a loose, round top that is sometimes flat and other times finished with a knot or tassel. This type of simple, pull-on hat has taken a leading position in head-gear for the growing girl, because it is simple in style and may be made out of the same material as the coat.   It comes under the class of tailored models because it is tailored in its construction rather than made by hand.

129. Variety in Tams.—Like all other types, the tam undergoes changes from season to season and produces as many different styles as are brought forth in any other shape.   Beginning with the original two-piece effect, tams have added piece after piece until at present we have tams made of ten and twelve sections.   This feature is excellent, particularly for utilizing left-over pieces.

When these different styles are in vogue, commercial patterns may be obtained at regular pattern counters.   However, the regulation two-piece type does not require a pattern because the head-size band is made just large enough to fit the child's head, and the top consists of a circular piece cut as large as is desired.   The top, which may be side-plaited or shirred to fit the head-size band, is often trimmed with a band of grosgrain ribbon, finished with a tailored bow or cocarde.

THREE-PIECE TAILORED TAM

130. Nature of Hat.—Next in popularity and simplicity to the regulation two-piece tam is the three-piece tailored tam shown in

Fig. 46.   This consists of a circular tip, a partly circular side crown with a seam at the back, and a 1½-inch head-size band.   The dimensions of this tam are: Head-size, 22 inches; tip, 13 inches; and circular side crown, 4¼ inches.

For its development, this model requires ½ yard of 40-inch material.

131. Making the Head-Size Band.—For the head-size band, join in a ring a strip of material, 4 inches wide and 23 inches long, by machine-stitching a ½-inch seam at the back.   Fold this ring through the center, making a band 2 inches wide, and machine-stitch along the folded edge.   Then, divide it into four equal parts and make notches to indicate the back, the front, and the sides.

132. Cutting the Tip.—For the tip, cut a circular piece of material 13½ inches in diameter, and make notches in it to indicate the front, the back, and the sides.

Fig. 46

133. Drafting the Side-Crown Pattern.—To develop the pattern for the partly circular side crown, as shown in Fig. 47, fold a sheet of paper 1½ inches longer and 6 inches wider than the tip, or 15 inches by 19½ inches, through the center, thus making an oblong piece 15 inches by 9¾ inches. Locate point a at the bottom and b at the top edge of the fold. Midway between a and b locate the point c, or the center of the fold.

On account of the cut-out portion at the back, and to bring this head-size opening in the proper line, 1 inch below point c locate point d, or the new center, and in line with this point on the open edge, locate point e. Along the bottom, from a measure 7½ inches along the edge and locate point·f.

So as to allow a ½-inch seam at the back, around the tip, and at the head-size, you will need a 5¼-inch side crown. Therefore, from point b on the top measure down 5¼ inches on the folded edge and locate point g. The distance from point g to d measures 3¼ inches, so to obtain the center back measure 3¼ inches below point d on the folded edge, and locate point h. Then, 3¼ inches to the right on a straight line with point h, locate point i. With a straight line, connect i and f or the center back.

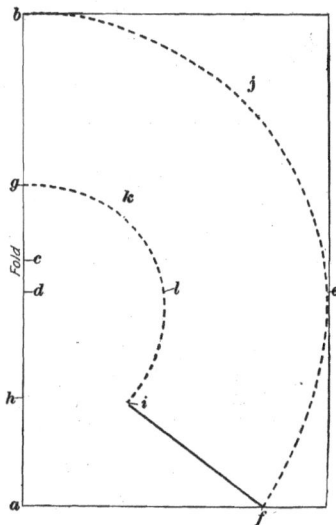

Fig. 47

134. With the direct front, the back, and the sides located, the next step is to locate the front diagonal points, which are half way between the front and the sides. The distance from d to b on the folded edge is 8½ inches and from d to e on the direct side is 9¾ inches. The diagonal point should measure one-half the difference between 8½ inches and 9¾ inches, more than the smaller measurement, or about 9¼ inches, in order to provide the right head-size to fit the band.

With the end of the ruler touching point d and the ruler resting on the upper right-hand corner, mark the diagonal point, as at j, 9¼ inches from d and, without removing the ruler, locate k, on the head-size line, 4 inches from *d*.   Next, with the ruler resting on *d* and *e*, make a mark 4½ inches from *d* and locate point *l* on the head-size line.

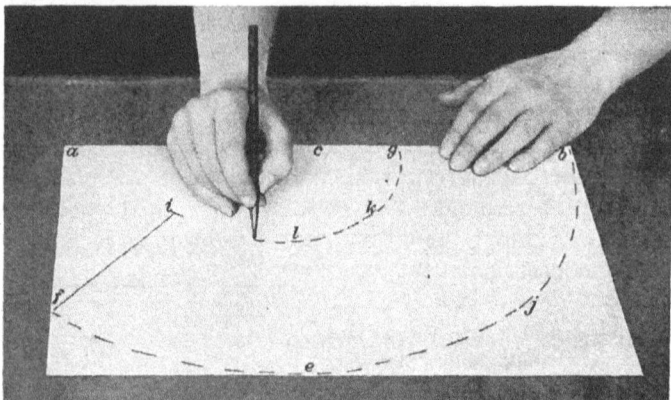

FIG. 48

135.   Next, connect *b*, *j*, and *e*, as shown in Fig. 48, with a free-hand, curved line, and continue with a slightly curved line to *f*, completing the outline of the outer edge of the side crown.   Then, beginning at the center front, or at *g*, with a free-hand curve connect *g*, *k*, *l*, and *i*, in the manner shown.

Cut along the outer edge and the head-size, or on the dotted lines, and on the back, or heavy, line *i*, to *f*, and before unfolding the pattern make notches at *b*, *e*, *g*, and *l* to indicate the front and the sides.   Then, lay the pattern on the material and cut the side crown with a ½-inch allowance for the back seam.

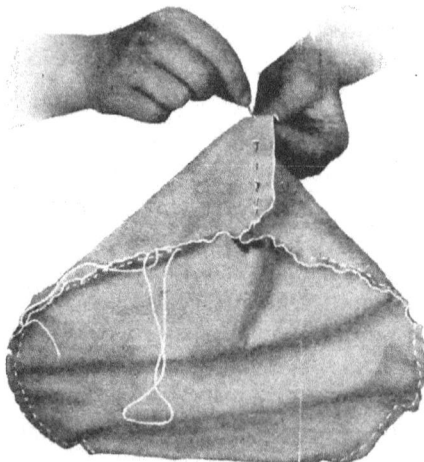

FIG. 49

136.   Assembling the Parts.—Attach the tip to the side crown by pinning the corresponding notches together; that is, the notches in the tip and the side crown that indicate the direct front and sides; then baste the seam around to about 2 inches from the back on each side, as shown in Fig. 49.   Next, pin the seam in the side crown.   After determining that the width of the seam is right to fit the remaining space of the tip, machine-stitch it, and press the seam flat.   Finish basting the side crown to the tip, machine-stitch the seam, and then remove the bastings.

Now slash the head-size opening with $\frac{1}{2}$-inch slashes and attach along one edge of the head-size band by pinning the notches together

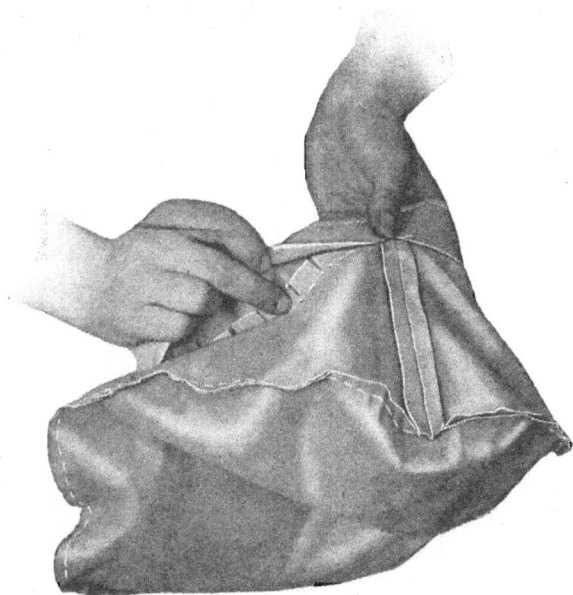

Fig. 50

and stitching.   Press the band and top seam with the tommy iron. Turn the inside edge down, as shown in Fig. 50, and baste; then stitch by machine with several rows of stitching.

Turn the tam right side out and it is ready for the trimming, which consists merely of a band of faille ribbon drawn around the crown and finished with a natty bow at the left side.

TUB HATS FOR TINY TOTS

NATURE OF TUB HATS

137. Along with the dainty, frilly dress models meant for "Sunday best," every growing girl requires a hat for general or rough-and-ready wear, particularly for the beach and country during vacation period. While the pressed body hats of patent milan, hemp, tagal, and rough braid are especially good for this use, they are inclined to appear heavy for midsummer wear because the majority of them are made in the dark staple colors. Therefore, the *tub hats*, so called because they are washable, find favor particularly for the little folks. Gingham, chambray, and brilliant cretonnes, together with dainty organdies, dotted Swiss, and embroidery, make both serviceable and adorable lingerie hats of this nature.

These hats are frameless, the brim depending for support on rows of machine stitching. Or wire, which can readily be removed for washing, may be inserted in the brim edge.

FLOPPY-BRIM, ENGLISH-PRINT HAT

138. For protection from the sun, the broad, even-brim, floppy hat shown in Fig. 51 cannot be excelled. It is made of English print, and has both its crown and its brim edged with a row of rickrack. The trimming consists of a band of colored organdie drawn through the slashes in the tam crown and finished with a pretty bow.

139. Material Requirements. To make the hat as it is illustrated, provide yourself with $\frac{3}{4}$ yard of 36-inch English print, 3 yards of rickrack braid, and $\frac{1}{8}$ yard of organdie.

FIG. 51

140. Making the Brim.—To make the brim, cut out two circular pieces of the material, 16 inches in diameter, and machine-stitch them together around the edge with a $\frac{1}{4}$-inch seam.   In the direct center, make a slash about 5 inches long and then turn the brim right side out.   Baste it securely along the edge; also, run several rows of bastings around the brim.   Then, run a row of machine stitching on the extreme edge and continue running rows in to the head-size, spacing them about $\frac{1}{4}$ inch apart and guiding the distance by the presser foot of the machine.   Stitching the hat in this manner causes a slight shrinkage in the material, so when the stitching is complete the brim will measure exactly 15 inches in diameter.

If the material used for this hat is light in weight, place a layer of tarlatan between the two parts of the brim; in most cases, though,

FIG. 52

a little starch added in the laundering will give sufficient stiffness.

To mark the head-size opening, lay a ribbon-wire, head-size band, the size of the wearer's head, on the center of the brim, pin securely, and pencil mark around the outside edge, as shown in Fig. 52.   About $\frac{3}{4}$ inch inside of this marking, cut the head-size and slash in tabs to the pencil mark.

To make a head-size band, cut a straight strip of the material, 3 inches wider and 1 inch longer than the head-size band, and join the ends in a ring with a $\frac{1}{2}$-inch seam; then fold this strip through the center and machine-stitch $\frac{1}{4}$ inch from the folded edge. Using the seam as the center back, apply this band in the manner

described for attaching the band in tailored tams.   To give it body
enough to stand up, run several rows of machine stitching around it.

Next, attach a row of rickrack around the edge of the brim by
means of machine stitching.

141.   Making the Crown.—For the crown, cut a circular piece
of material, 14½ inches in diameter, and machine-stitch a tiny hem
on the extreme edge.   Then, ½ inch from the edge, at intervals of
about 3½ inches, put in 2-inch vertical rows of hemstitching and cut
these to make slashes that will come just under the box plaits.   Next,
sew a row of rickrack around the edge of the crown.   Now lay the
box plaits at intervals around the crown, which can then be sewed
to the head-size band underneath the plaits.

142.   Trimming.—A strip of white lawn or organdie, 4 inches
wide and 1⅜ yards long, forms the very simple and appropriate
trimming.   Have it hemstitched for picoting on the edge and ends,
draw it through the slashes underneath the plaits, and then finish it
with a tight bow.

TUB POKE

143.   Nature of Hat.—The quaint little poke shown in Fig. 53
is another type of fabric tub hat.   It is made of ⅝ yard of 36-inch

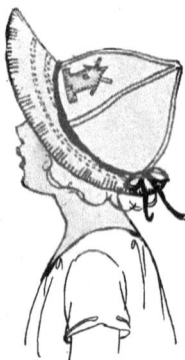

chambray, and is trimmed with buttonhole-
stitches and an appliquéd windmill motif cut out
of linen or piqué.   This model is made in a way
similar to the one just described, but before the
material is cut it is well to develop a paper
pattern.

144.   Drafting the Brim Pattern.—For the
brim, cut a circular piece of paper 16 inches in
diameter, cut out the head-size, slash the brim
at the back, and lap it so that the slashed edges
extend on each side, making a lap of about
3 inches, which will draw the sides down and
pull the back in close to the head.   Trim the

Fig. 53

head-size and the outer edge until the brim measures 1½ inches at
the back, 2¾ inches at the sides, and 3⅜ inches in the front.   Also,
trim the lapped edges to allow for a ¼-inch seam at the back.

145.   Making the Brim.—Lay this pattern on two thicknesses
of material, cut out the brim, allowing an extra ½ inch for the seam

on the edge.   After stitching this seam, open out the two thicknesses so that they lie flat and make a $\frac{1}{4}$-inch seam at the back.   Then turn the brim right side out, and baste around the edge.

The stitching in this hat is a little different from that in the previous one; that is, it is stitched in sections, two rows in each section, as shown.

146.   Completing the Hat.—After the brim has been stitched, adjust the head-size to the head-size band, made as explained in Art. **131.**   Then, make a four-piece sectional crown, shaping it up in an extreme point at the center top.

Cut the windmill design out of contrasting material and appliqué it on one of the sections by means of the buttonhole-stitch; also, finish the outer edge of the brim with long and short buttonhole-stitches.   Then, draw a narrow ribbon or a strip of self-material around the crown and finish in a bow at the back.

TUCKED MODEL

147.   Nature of Hat.—Nothing could be smarter for the little miss whose span of years does not exceed five, than the dainty lingerie hat shown in Fig. 54.   Batiste, organdie, or lawn may be used in developing this model, white being chosen for general wear but a color being very desirable to match a pretty summer dress.   In this case, the materials used were $\frac{3}{4}$ yard of organdie, 1 yard of insertion, $1\frac{3}{4}$ yards of lace, and $1\frac{1}{2}$ yards of ribbon.

FIG. 54

148.   Dimensions.—The dimensions of this hat are: Head-size, $21\frac{1}{2}$ inches; width of brim, 3 inches; and length of edge, 40 inches.

149.   Making the Brim.—For the brim, use a 4-inch-wide strip of organdie, which has been pin-tucked $\frac{1}{2}$ inch apart and measures $40\frac{1}{2}$ inches in length after the tucking is done.   Join the ends of this strip in a ring and make a $\frac{1}{2}$-inch hem or casing along one edge for a wire, leaving about 1 inch for an opening at the direct back.   Cut a piece of No. 21 brace wire, 40 inches long, and run it through this casing, joining the ends with a clip at the back.   Then, close the opening by stitching with a few fine overcasting-stitches.

Apply the Val-lace frill by stitching it along the row of machine stitching.

Next, make a 21½-inch head-size band as described for the hat in Fig. 50. Cut along the inside edge of the brim material to make the brim measure 3½ inches wide and run a shirr string ½ inch from the edge. Apply the head-size band around the row of shirring.

150. Making the Crown.—For the soft, tam-effect, sectional crown, pin-tuck a 9-inch-wide strip of organdie, making a strip 32 inches long. To develop a pattern, divide a regulation oval

FIG. 55

crown into four equal parts and cut a pattern of one section, adding about 1 inch around the edges for fulness. Lay this pattern on the tucked material so that the tucks run crosswise and cut four sections.

Join two of the sections with a strip of Val insertion, and then join the other two in the same manner. Next, join these two sides with a strip of insertion running from front to back. Turn a ¼-inch seam in around the head-size and run a row of shirring along this.

Apply the crown to the head-size band and finish with a band of No. 5 ribbon, ending it in a bow at the left side.

151.   Preparation for Laundering.—To launder this hat, remove the crown, open the hand-stitched portion of the wire casing at the back, loosen the clip, and draw the wire out, as shown in Fig. 55.

_____

SOFT, WIRELESS HAT

152.   Nature of Hat.—For the tiny tot, where comfort is of chief importance, all rigid lines are practically barred, and hats made decidedly soft, with brims unsupported, are much preferred.   The model shown in Fig. 56 is a hat of this kind, it being developed out of batiste and Val lace and made so that it is all in one piece and can therefore be laundered very easily.

FIG. 56

153.   Cutting the Material.—To copy this hat, cut a piece of batiste 13 inches wide and 30 inches long, join the ends to form a ring, and divide the ring into four equal parts, the seam being used for the direct back.   On the top edge, beginning at the center back, about 1 inch from the edge, cut off a strip, graduating this strip out to nothing at each side.   On the bottom edge, cut off a similar strip.   This makes the material narrower at the back than in front.

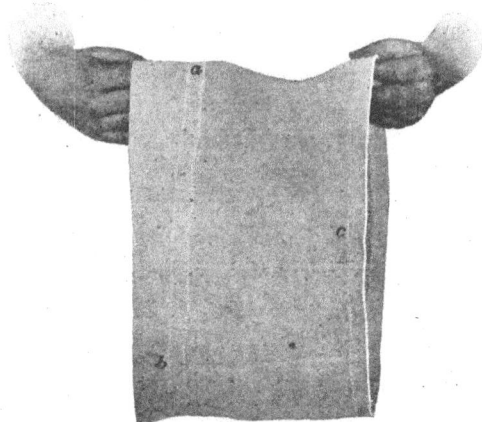

FIG. 57

154.   Finishing the Edge.—Next, turn the bottom edge in about 2½ inches in front and graduate the turning to about 1¾ inches at the back. Machine-stitch this hem and make a casing ¼ inch wide, as at

_a_, Fig. 57, for a shirring tape.   Note that the hem at point _a_ is wider than at _b_, which is the back of the hat

As a finish for the top edge, make a ¾-inch hem, as shown at *c*. Hemstitch a row of the Val lace on the lower edge to serve as a finish. The lace frill, caused by hemstitching the lace on the edge, gives it a dainty, softening effect.

155. Finishing the Hat.—Sew a row of beading directly over the casing that is to serve as the head-size, and one on the top edge, and run a band of pink faille No. 5 ribbon through both strips of beading. In sewing the beading on the top edge; it is necessary to run only one row of stitching at *e*, allowing the other edge to be loose so that it will stand out when the ribbon is drawn up.

Run a shirring tape or a narrow elastic through the casing at the head-size to make it fit the head and run a shirring tape in the top. Then, draw the ribbon up through the beading at the head-size and make a small bow at the left side. Also, draw up the shirring tape in the top as tight as possible and draw up the ribbon, making, at the right side, a bow that has ends in streamer fashion.

MILLINERY FOR MISSES AND CHILDREN

EXAMINATION QUESTIONS

(1) To create appropriate millinery for juveniles, what must the designer possess?

(2) What three requisites should characterize hats for misses and children?

(3) (a) In making hats for tiny tots, how are the head-sizes governed?
(b) Why is the measurement from ear to ear taken?

(4) How do hats for juveniles compare with those designed for the grown-up sister?

(5) Why is the width of the brim an essential consideration in the selecting of hats for growing girls?

(6) (a) What is the most desirable trimming arrangement for misses and children? (b) What type of frame is considered most becoming to the very youthful?

(7) (a) Describe the manner in which the braid is sewed on the brim of the model in Fig. 4. (b) How are the rings made that are used in the trimming?

(8) Why are several ½-inch slashes made in the petals used on the brim of the model in Fig. 6?

(9) (a) Why is the foundation crown in Fig. 14 cut away? (b) How may the joining of the plaited Val lace on the hat in Fig. 16 be hidden?

(10) Where is the edge wire attached on the hat shown in Fig. 18 if the brim is inclined to ripple?

(11) Describe the way in which the collar effect around the crown in Fig. 25 is made.

(12) (a) How is the brim in Fig. 30 made to assume a broad, off-the-face shape? (b) Why is the fulness of the shirred edge pushed around to the sides?

§ 10

(13) (*a*) What is a bolera shape? (*b*) How is the material for the brim in Fig. 32 cut?

(14) In what manner does the cloche shown in Fig. 40 differ from the frame shown in Fig. 39?

(15) How is the variation of the cloche obtained in Fig. 45?

(16) (*a*) What is the tam shown in Fig. 46 called? (*b*) Draft a pattern of the side crown and send it.

(17) What material is used in developing the hat shown in Fig. 51?

(18) Describe the way in which a pattern may be made for the brim of the hat shown in Fig. 53.

(19) How is the hat shown in Fig. 54 prepared for laundering?

(20) How is the material cut for the hat shown in Fig. 56?

www.ingramcontent.com/pod-product-compliance
Lightning Source LLC
Chambersburg PA
CBHW031055280326
41928CB00047B/348